The Official Rules
at
WORK

**Other Official Rules Books
by Paul Dickson
Published by Walker and Company**

The Official Rules at Home

The Official Rules

at

WORK

*The Principles, Maxims, and Instructions
That Define Your Life
on the Job*

Paul Dickson

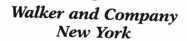

**Walker and Company
New York**

First published in the United States of America in 1996 by Walker Publishing Company, Inc.

Published simultaneously in Canada by
Thomas Allen & Son Canada, Limited, Markham, Ontario

Library of Congress Cataloging-in-Publication Data
   The official rules at work: the principles, maxims, and instructions that define your life on the job/[compiled by]Paul Dickson.
      p. cm.
   Includes index.
   ISBN 0-8027-1317-3
   1. American wit and humor.   I. Paul Dickson.
PN6162.D49 1996
818'.540208—dc20   96-12064 CIP

Book design by James McGuire

Printed in the United States of America

10 9 8 7 6 5 4 3 2 1

The Official Rules

at

WORK

CALAMITAS NECESSARIA EST

Introduction

It started simply. In 1976 the compiler of this work created something called The Murphy Center for the Codification of Human and Organizational Law. It was mainly inspired by Murphy's Law ("If anything can go wrong, it will") and influenced by the fact that we had put men on the moon but still seemed unable to create shoelaces that didn't break at inopportune moments. Originally nothing more than a shoe box stuffed with rules, laws, and modern maxims, the Center has to date received more than 7,000 letters, published three books and a gaggle of magazine articles of its findings, and been dubbed "the world's smallest think tank."

Currently spanning a dozen shoe boxes and a filing cabinet, The Murphy Center endeavors to collect, test, and make a few bucks from the revealed truths that are often the by-product of what the Center likes to think of fondly as O.F.F.M. & G.C., or Other Folks' Foibles, Misfortunes, and General Confusion.

These are good times for the Center, which thrives on turmoil and discombobulation. It has already outlived such temporary institutions as the World Football League, World Communism, the Cold War, the Berlin Wall, an assortment of airlines, the V-8 engine, scores of financial institutions, and a host of other ephemera. It has watched AT&T break up twice (1982 and 1996), watched several baseball strikes—each more self-destructive than the one before—and watched the level of political discourse drop every two years.

Now entering a new phase, the Center is creating a series of special collections, each one tailored to a different realm of human existence. *The Official Rules at Home*, this book's companion volume, takes on home and family life.

The laws that follow explain such diverse and seemingly inexplicable phenomena as office machines, bureaucracies, bosses, expense accounts, government regulation, hierarchies, meetings, committees, and watercooler politics. This book is for everyone who works, from managers to the rank and file, and small-business owners to the self-employed. It contains the best and most relevant rules—many never published before in book form——that govern (and offer insight into) our working lives. The purpose of this collection is not merely to amuse but to be useful to all of us who work for a living.

The rules appear in the exact language of the person who discovered the phenomenon or universal truth, including their name for that discovery. Every attempt has been made to find the original author of each discovery, but, sadly, some appear as "unknown origin."

The items were collected over a period of years and are listed alphabetically by name of the law, effect, or principle. This gives them a sense of the categorical and chronological randomness that approximates the randomness of our workaday world.

In addition to the main body of the book, there are several special bonus sections from The Murphy Center that, it is hoped, will allow us all to better understand how things at work really *work*.

Enough preamble. Here are the rules, maxims, principles, and instructions that define your life on the job.

A

- **Accounting, The Four Laws of.** (1) Trial balances don't. (2) Working capital doesn't. (3) Liquidity tends to run out. (4) Return on investments never will.

> —Anonymous

- **Acheson's Comment on Experts.** An expert is like a eunuch in a harem—someone who knows all about it but can't do anything about it.

> —Dean Acheson; from Theodore C. Achilles

- **Ackley's Axiom.** The degree of technical competence is inversely proportional to the level of management.

> —Bob Ackley, T. Sgt., USAF, Plattsmouth, Nebraska. He adds, "Originally defined—in 1967—as 'The level of intelligence is inversely proportional to the number of stripes,' then I had to modify it as I accrued more stripes."

• **Ackley's Latest Finding.** If you are a big enough company, your mistakes become standards.
> —Bob Ackley, Plattsmouth, Nebraska, who has dedicated this finding to IBM

• **Addis's Admonitions.** (1) If it don't fit in a pigeonhole, maybe it ain't a pigeon. (2) Never play cat-and-mouse games if you're a mouse. (3) Ambiguity is the first refuge of the wrong. (4) The shadow of your goalpost is better than no shade at all.
> —Don Addis, St. Petersburg, Florida

• **Addis's Business Wisdom.** (1) Any given company policy, rules, or procedure will outlast everybody's memory of why it was instituted. (2) If at first you don't succeed, redefine success.
> —Don Addis, St. Petersburg, Florida, cartoonist and columnist for the *St. Petersburg Times,* whose first rule of humor is "If you're going to joke—be funny."

• **Adkins's Rule of Milk and Other Precious Commodities.** The less you have, the more you spill.
> —Betsy Adkins, Gardiner, Maine

• **Advertising Admonition.** In writing a patent medicine advertisement, first convince the reader that he has the disease he is reading about; second, that it is curable.

—R. F. Fenno, 1908

• **Advice to Officers of the British Army.** (1) Ignorance of your profession is likewise best concealed by solemnity and silence, which pass for profound knowledge upon the generality of mankind. A proper attention to these, together with extreme severity, particularly in trifles, will soon procure you the character of a good officer. (2) As you probably did not rise to your present distinguished rank by your own merit, it cannot reasonably be expected that you should promote others on that score. (3) Be sure to give out a number of orders. . . . The more trifling they are, the more it shows your attention to the service; and should your orders contradict one another, it will give you an opportunity of altering them, and find subject for fresh regulations.

—Discovered by Stuart G. Vogt of Clarksville, Tennessee, who has a copy of the sixth edition of the small book titled *Advice to the Officers of the British Army,* published in 1783

• **Air Force Inertia Axiom.** Consistency is always easier to defend than correctness.

—Anonymous; from Russell Fillers, Bethel, Connecticut

• **Alan's Theorem.** In any group of eagles, you will find some turkeys.

> —Alan B. Guerrina,
> Woodbridge, Virginia

• **Allcock's Law of Communication.** The time that passes before you hear about an event is in direct proportion to the extent to which it affects you.

> —John Allcock, University of
> Bradford, Bradford, West
> Yorkshire, England

• **Allen's Reassurance.** He's got more talent in his whole body than you've got in your little finger.

> —Gracie Allen, heard on the
> rebroadcast of an old radio
> show, WAMU, Washington, D.C.

• **Allen's Rule of Universal Constancy.** The only thing constant in the Navy is the varying rate of change.

> —From Daniel K. Snyder, Pearl
> City, Hawaii, who attributes it to
> Bob Allen and adds, "Codified at
> the Fleet Ballistic Missile
> Training Center in Charleston,
> South Carolina, in early 1977,
> but since that time found to be
> applicable not only to the Navy,
> but to the world in general"

- **Allen's Tenet.** The strength of one's opinion on any matter in controversy is inversely proportional to the amount of knowledge that the person has on that subject.

>   —Patrick J. Allen, Chicago, Illinois

- **Aman's Discovery.** Management is always trying to fine-tune the solution before it defines the problem.

>   —Wayne Aman, Burnsville, Minnesota

- **Ames's Working Hypothesis.** The self-employed person is uniquely in a position to define success however he pleases.

>   —Mary E. Ames, *Washington Post*, March 6, 1983

- **Amis's Admonition.** You can't believe anyone but yourself; and don't trust yourself too completely.

>   —Jim Amis, Springfield, Missouri

- **Amos's Law.** All my ideas are good; it's only the people who put them into practice that aren't.

>   —The character Amos Brearly in the British television series "Emmerdale Farm"; from Peter Scott, Portsmouth, England

• **Amundsen's Discovery.** Victory awaits those who have everything in order. People call this luck.
—Polar explorer Roald
Amundsen; from M. L. Smith

• **Anonymous's Contribution to the National Security Debate.** The difference between the military and the Boy Scouts of America is that the Boy Scouts are allowed to carry knives and they have adult leadership.
—Found by Lt. Col. N. E. Kass,
Fort Walton Beach, Florida

• **Anonymous's Reminder to Mind the Real Objective.** Why worry about low tire pressure when you're out of gas.
—Anon., Santa Ana, California

• **Anthony's Songs of the Desk Jockey.** (1) The federal government spends enough in one hour to wire the entire population of North Dakota—and the houses, too. (2) Discriminate as little as you can and still comply with federal regulations. (3) The principal allegiance of modern man is to his group, which differs from a gang chiefly in that gangs rumble in the streets while groups rumble in the courts and on Capitol Hill. (4) A dresser is a kind of bureau that doesn't tell you how to run your life. (5) The fascination of paper clips grows inversely with the appeal of the work at hand.
—Ryan Anthony, Tucson,
Arizona

• **The Apotheosis Assumption.** The boss already has the right answers.
> —Sidney I. Riskin, Tarrytown, New York

• **Armitage's Finding.** Anything put off this morning, will reach critical mass during lunch break.
> —R. Armitage, Scunthorpe, England

• **Arnold's Square Wheel Theory.** A prevalent form of decision-making holds that if three out of four schools, firms, or whatever are using square wheels, then the fourth will follow.
> —Richard Arnold, Keezletown, Virginia

• **Aronfy's Law of the Post Office.** The likelihood of a letter getting lost in the mail is directly proportional to its importance.
> —Andrew G. Aronfy, M.D., Seabrook, Maryland

B

• **Banks's Revision.** If at first you do succeed—
try to hide your astonishment.
> —Harry F. Banks

• **Bastl's Law.** Through many years of diligence,
perseverance, and hard work, one can successfully
maintain one's position at the bottom of one's profession.
> —James F. Bastl, Westchester,
> Illinois. (Originally published in
> the *Chicago Tribune*, November
> 20, 1983.)

• **Batt's Laws.** (1) Once you overcome your fear
of public speaking, you'll never be asked to speak
again. (2) The long-winded person will always
answer your long-distance calls.
> —Al Batt, Hartland, Minnesota

• **BB's Group Dynamics Dictum.** In a group,
the unknowing will try to teach the lesser-skilled
or-knowing.
> —Bruce "BB" Brown, Mar Vista,
> California

• **Belle's Constant.** The ratio of time involved in work to time available for work is usually about 0:6.

> —From a 1977 *Journal of Irreproducible Results* article of the same title by Daniel McIvor and Olsen Belle, in which it is observed that knowledge of this constant is most useful in planning long-range projects. It is based on such things as an analysis of an eight-hour workday in which only 4.8 hours are actually spent working (or 0.6 of the time available), with the rest being spent on coffee breaks, bathroom visits, resting, walking, fiddling around, and trying to determine what to do next.

• **Benchley's Law.** Anyone can do any amount of work, provided it isn't the work he is supposed to be doing at that moment.

> —Robert Benchley, from his essay "How to Get Things Done"

• **Bender's Laws.** (1) No two office machines are compatible. (2) In word processing, the worst typos remain invisible until the printout. If the typo also creates an error in fact, it will remain invisible until the letter is in the mail.

> —Georgia Bender, Kittanning, Pennsylvania

• **Bentov's Law.** One's level of ignorance increases exponentially with accumulated knowledge. For example, when one acquires a bit of new information, there are many new questions that are generated by it, and each new piece of information breeds five or ten new questions. These questions pile up at a much faster rate than does the accumulated information. The more one knows, therefore, the greater his level of ignorance.

> —Itsahak Bentov, from *Stalking the Wild Pendulum*, 1977; from Neal Wilgus

• **Berla's Version.** If you file it, you'll never need it. If you need it, you never file it.

> —Michael Berla, Columbia, Maryland

• **Bernstein's Principle of Homogeneity.** Behavior and personality traits are relatively constant even in very different situations and relationships. *Corollary 1:* You can't be one kind of person and another kind of president. *Corollary 2:* You can't be a wonderful friend and an abusive parent. *Corollary 3:* Someone who treats a relative fairly will do the same with a stranger.

> —Barbara Bernstein, Bowie, Maryland

• **Beshere's Formula for Failure.** There are only two kinds of people who fail: those who listen to

nobody, and . . . those who listen to everybody.
>—Thomas M. Beshere, Jr.,
>Charleston, South Carolina

• **Bethell's Iron Law of Conferences.** The number in attendance diminishes with time.
>—Tom Bethell, *National Review*,
>November 25, 1988

• **Beville's Rule of Secrecy in Business.** Secrecy is the enemy of efficiency, but don't let anyone know it.
>—Richard Beville, London,
>England

• **Blake's Law.** Anything that can change, is.
>—Kathleen Blake, Dallas,Texas;
>from F. D. McSpiritt

• **Blumenthal's Observation.** The difference between business and government is that the government has no bottom line.
>—Secretary of the Treasury W.
>Michael Blumenthal; from
>Theodore C. Achilles

• **Blutarsky's Axiom.** Nothing is impossible for the man who will not listen to reason.
>—The character Blutarsky,
>played by John Belushi, in the
>movie *Animal House*.

• **Bone's Labor Discovery.** Unlimited manpower can solve any problem except what to do with the manpower; for example, if a man can dig a hole in a minute, why can't sixty men dig a hole in one second?

> —Jonathan Bone, Chicago, Illinois

• **Boren's Laws of the Bureaucracy.** (1) When in doubt, mumble. (2) When in trouble, delegate. (3) When in charge, ponder.

> —James H. Boren, founder, president, and chairperson of the board of the International Association of Professional Bureaucrats (INATAPROBU)

• **Boston's Discovery.** Cash flow is an oxymoron.

> —Bruce Boston, Fairfax, Virginia

• **Boyd's Managerial Survival Law #1.** When faced with a crisis, take the inevitable and turn it around to make it look like a conscious decision.

> —Richard D. Boyd, Ukiah, California

• **Boyle's Laws Applicable to the Workplace.** (1) Your career will unfold as a series of miscalculations, not all yours. (2) Your future will depend upon having the courage of your miscalculations. (3) If they discover your standards, they will use them against you. (4) If you gain the doctorate, you will lose your first name. (5) Today's disaster is tomorrow's archaeology. (6) It is possible to make the right mistake. (7) Every life is a solo flight. (8) The ears have walls.

> —Charles P. Boyle, Annapolis, Maryland

• **Brady's Law of Problem Solving.** When confronted by an unseemingly difficult problem, it is easier solved by reducing it to the question "How would the Lone Ranger have handled this?"

> —Karyn Brady, Phoenix, Arizona

• **Branch's Law of Crisis.** The spirit of public service will rise, and the bureaucracy will multiply itself much faster, in time of grave national concern.

> —Taylor Branch, from his March 1974 article in *Harper's* titled "The Sunny Side of the Energy Crisis"

• **Brecht's Reminder.** As a grown man you should know better than to go around advising people.

> —Bertolt Brecht; from Bernard L. Albert

• **Brennan's Laws.** (1) Pay Expectancy. Everyone wants to be paid exactly what they are worth, as long as it is more than they are making. (2) Cost of Living. When the cost of living goes up, people expect pay to go down. When the cost of living goes down, people expect pay to stay up. (3) Consulting. When management concludes that someone from the outside is always smarter than an employee, they are telling their employees that no one with any brains could be expected to work here.

> —E. James Brennan, Brennan-Thomsen Associates, Chesterfield, Missouri

• **Brenner's Location Is Everything Rule.** If you want to run with the big dogs, you've got to go potty in the tall grass.

> —The late Glenn Brenner, Washington, D.C., television sports anchor, quoted in the *Washington Post*, March 15, 1986

• **Brewer's Reminder.** Don't start vast projects with half-vast ideas.

> —Bill Brewer, Annandale, Virginia, who saw this admonition on a sign while working at NACA (the forerunner of NASA) at Langley Field, Virginia, around 1957

- **Brien's First Law.** At some time in the life cycle of virtually every organization, its ability to succeed in spite of itself runs out.
> —Richard H. Brien, "The Managerialization of Higher Education," from *Educational Record*, Summer 1970

- **Brower's Aphorism.** Honesty is not only the best policy, it is rare enough today to make you pleasantly conspicuous.
> —Charles Brower; from a set of aphorisms he composed in 1970 when he retired from post as chairman of BBDO, the advertising giant

- **Brown's Aphorism.** Nothing worth learning is learned quickly except parachuting. *Brown's Postulate:* No matter how low your own self-esteem, there are probably others who think less of you. *Brown's Point:* One of the virtues of propaganda is that it is easy to understand. *Brown's Revision:* Man does not breed by love alone.
> —Professor David S. Brown, Washington, D.C., from a much larger collection

• **Brown's Law.** Too often I find that the volume of paper expands to fill the available briefcases.
> —Governor Jerry Brown, quoted in *State Government News*, March 1973

• **Brown's Law of Business Success.** Our customer's paperwork is profit. Our own paperwork is loss.
> —Tony Brown, programmer at the Control Data Corporation

• **Brown's Laws.** (1) A memo longer than one page no longer is a memo. (2) Your self-imagined importance is in direct proportion to the illegibility of your signature. (3) Anything written to another person is sure to (a) end up in someone else's hands; (b) be misunderstood, and (c) be photocopied.
> —David H. Brown, President, Brown-Speak Communications, Rockville, Maryland

• **Brownian Motion Rule of Bureaucracies.** It is impossible to distinguish, from a distance, whether the bureaucrats associated with your project are simply sitting on their hands or frantically trying to cover their asses.
> —Unknown origin; submitted by Paul Martin to Donald R. Woods

• **Brozik's Laws.** (1) In any organization, it is more important to pick your enemies than it is to pick your friends. (2) Never buy anything expensive from somebody who dresses better than you do. One of you is playing in the wrong league.

> —Dallas Brozik, Huntington, West Virginia

• **Budget Analyst's Rule.** Distribute dissatisfaction uniformly.

> —A. A. Lidberg, Tempe, Arizona

• **Buffett's Poker Principle.** If you've been in the game thirty minutes and you don't know who the patsy is, *you're* the patsy.

> —Warren E. Buffett, chairman of Berkshire Hathaway, Inc., quoted in the *New York Times*, April 5, 1988, from Joseph C. Goulden

BUFFET'S POKER PRINCIPLE

• **Burdg's Philosophy.** It's not the time you put in, but what you put in the time.
> —Henry B. Burdg, Auburn, Alabam

• **Bureaucratic Bylaw of Deliverance.** God told Moses he had good news and bad news.

"The good news first," said Moses.

"I'm planning to part the Red Sea to allow you and your people to walk right through and escape from Egypt," said God, adding, "and when the Egyptian soldiers pursue, I'll send the water back on top of them."

"Wonderful," Moses responded, "but what's the bad news?"

"You write the environmental-impact statement."
> —Oft-told Washington parable, ca. 1977

• **Bureau Termination, Law of.** When a government bureau is scheduled to be phased out, the number of employees in that bureau will double within twelve months after that decision is made.
> —James A. Cassidy, Philadelphia, Pennsylvania

• **Burgy's Definition of Statistics.** A bunch of numbers running around looking for an argument.
> —George Burgy, Rockville, Maryland

- **Burnham's Tenth Law.** If there's no alternative, there's no problem.
  —James Burnham

- **Burns's Lament.** Too bad that all the people who know how to run the country are busy driving taxicabs and cutting hair.
  —George Burns

- **Busch's Law of the Forty-Hour Week.** The closer a day is to a weekend, holiday, or vacation, the greater the probability of an employee calling in sick. *Corollary:* No one gets sick on Wednesdays.
  —Walter Busch, St. Louis, Missouri; from Elaine Viets

- **Butler's Expert Testimony.** The function of the expert is not to be more right than other people, but to be wrong for more sophisticated reasons.
  —David Butler, *The Observer*, London, England

- **Butler's Marketing Principle.** Any fool can paint a picture, but it takes a wise man to be able to sell it.
  —Samuel Butler

- **Byars's Bylaws.** (1) Never work for a boss who opens the company mail. (2) The customer is always right . . . and ignored.
  —Betty Joe Byars, High Point, North Carolina

C

• **Caffyn's Law of "According to."** The rosier the news, the higher-ranking the official who announces it.

> —H. R. Caffyn, New York, New York; from Alan L. Otten

• **Canfield's Corollary to the "You Can't Win 'em All Rule":** You can't even fight 'em all.

> —Monte Canfield, formerly of the General Accounting Office; from Sharon Lynn, Washington, D.C.

• **Carlisle's Rule.** To find the IQ of any committee or commission, first determine the IQ of the most stupid member and then divide that result by the number of members.

> —Carlisle Madson, Hopkins, Minnesota

• **Carswell's Law of Productivity.** Work smarter, not harder.

> —Ron Carswell, Texas State Technical Institute, Waco

• **Carvlin's Commentaries.** The risk in a business venture should not seriously outweigh the prospective reward, as, for example, in picking a policeman's pocket.

—Tom Carvlin, Dolton, Illinois

• **Cason's Laws.** (1) *For Plant Operation:* When in doubt, blame the Maintenance Department. (2) *For Economic Analysis:* The assumption you make without realizing you are making it is the one that will do you in. (3) *For Speed Limitation:* They will remember how poorly the job was done long after they have forgotten how quickly it was done. (4) *For Meetings:* Regardless of the length of the meeting, all important decisions will be made in the last five minutes before lunch or quitting time.

—Rober L. Cason, Wilmington, Delaware

• *Cavalry Journal* **Discovery.** A staff study is a record of the tortuous thought processes between a set of invalid assumptions and a foregone conclusion.

—From a mid-1930s issue of that journal; from Jerry Cowan

• **Cavanagh's Laws of Bureaucratic Management.** (1) The process is the substance. (2) The staff is the line.

—Richard E. Cavanagh, Washington, D.C.

• **Celine's Laws.** (1) National security is the chief cause of national insecurity. (2) Accurate communication is possible only in a nonpunishing situation. (3) An honest politician is a national calamity.

> —Hagbard Celine, in Robert Anton Wilson's *Iluminati Papers;* from Neal Wilgus

• **Charnovitz's Postulate for Elevators.** The fewer the floors an elevator has to serve, the more time it takes for the elevator to travel between each floor.

> —Steve Charnovitz, Falls Church, Virginia

• **Chilton's Theological-Clerical Rule.** If you work in a church office you have to keep all your equipment locked up, because nothing is sacred.

> —Vee Chilton, Easton, Maryland

• **Chism's Law of Completion.** The amount of time required to complete a government project is precisely equal to the amount of time already spent on it.

> —Shelby Chism, Overland Park, Kansas

• **Civil Service Maxim (a.k.a., The Law of the "New Army").** The pension is mightier than the sword.

> —Anonymous; from an unsigned note sent to The Murphy Center

• **C.J.'s Law.** Philosophy doesn't get the washing-up done.

> —The character C. J. in the British TV series "The Rise and Fall of Reggie Perrin"; from Shel Kagan

• **Clark's Clamor.**
Where are they?
How many were they?
Which way were they going?
I must find them.
I am their leader.

> —From Bob Kerr, Amarillo, Texas, who spotted this sign on the office wall of Hugh Clark

• **Clark's Law of Leadership.** A leader should not get too far in front of his troops or he will get shot in the ass.

> —Senator Joseph S. Clark

• **Clarke's Law.** Improving something is admirable, but inevitably five times zero is still zero.

> —Dean Travis Clarke, Glen Cove, New York

• **Clay's Conclusion.** If you ever saw a cat and a dog eating out of the same plate, you can bet your ass it was the cat's food.
>—Rep. William Clay (D.-Mo.), commenting on the suggestion that public employee unions form a coalition with Jimmy Carter in 1980; from Marshall L. Smith

• **Clifton's Advice.** Don't give up high ground till you know you're over the pass.
>—Kelly H. Clifton, Hiroshima, Japan, who says that it was derived from backpacking but seems to have wider application

• **Collins's Law of Control.** Businesses exert the tightest controls over the easiest things to control, rather than the most critical.
>—Kenneth B. Collins, CBS Publications, New York, New York

• **Combs's Laws.** (1) A lot of people who complain about their boss being stupid would be out of a job if he were any smarter. (2) If you think OSHA is a small town in Wisconsin, you're in trouble.
>—M. C. "Chuck" Combs, Director, Minnesota Department of Agriculture, Marketing Services, St. Paul, Minnesota

- **Condon's Laws.** *Business Eating:* The cost of an expense-account lunch is always inversely proportional to the amount of business done.
Responsibility: The thickness of the Chief Executive's carpet is in direct proportion to the amount of buck-passing carried out.

—John Condon, Dublin, Ireland

- **Connolly's Law of Cost Control.** The price of any product produced for a government agency will be not less than the square of the initial Firm Fixed-Price Contract.

—Ray Connolly, in *Electronics* magazine

- **Conway's Law.** In any organization there will always be one person who knows what is going on. That person must be fired.

—Letters column in the *New York Times*, May 15, 1980; from Robert W. Sallen

- **Joe Cooch's Laws.** (1) If things are military and make sense, coincidence has entered the picture. (2) To hell with the content, let's get the format straight. (3) Personnel officers exist primarily for the purpose of screwing up other people's careers. (4) The most complicated problems always arise at the most remote locations. (5) Writing a directive and getting people to pay attention to it are two entirely different operations. (6) Staff studies should always be written in support of foregone conclusions; assumptions will be furnished later. (7) The more esoteric the presentation, the thicker the accept of the person presenting it. (8) Generals must be kept busy or their subordinates will be. (9) Greatest consideration in personnel matters is given to those individuals who are the least efficient and the most troublesome; or, if you want top-level support, screw up. (10) It is illegal for any headquarters to admit error. (11) Planners are people who take implausible assumptions, apply these to conditions that could not possibly exist, using resources that will undoubtedly not be available, to produce a plan of action that is inconceivable to be followed out. (12) One thousand guesses added together are not necessarily more accurate than one big guess. (13) The longer you work on a casualty estimate, the less accurate it becomes. (14) If people don't obey a Regulation, write another more complicated. (15) Invariably, the least knowledgeable of individuals is the most vocal.

—The late Joe Cooch, Medical Corps, U.S. Army, was a widely known Army Medical Department Preventive Medicine Officer. Examples of adaptations of Joe Cooch's code to fields outside the military (scientific research, for one) are common.

• **Cooke's Fundamental Theorem of Political Economics.** If you can only cover costs, capitalism is irrelevant.

> —Ernest F. Cooke, Chairman,
> Marketing Department,
> University of Baltimore

• **Coolidge's Immutable Observation.** When more and more people are thrown out of work, unemployment results.

> —Calvin Coolidge; from Leonard
> C. Lewin's *Treasury of American
> Political Humor*, Dial, 1964

• **Cossey's Advice.** Instead of starting at the bottom and working up, people should start at the top and work down. Only when one knows the job above can the one below be done correctly.

> —Clarence Cossey, Austin, Texas

• **Cox's Realization.** The prediction that will be fulfilled is the one you didn't have the nerve to voice.

> —Richard Cox, Vandalia, Illinois

• **Crenna's Law of Accountability.** If you are the first to know about something bad, you are going to be held responsible for acting on it, regardless of your formal duties.

> —C. D. Crenna, policy adviser,
> Ottawa, Ontario, Canada

• **Crescimbeni's Rule on Working.** Don't worry about people not working at their jobs in the afternoons. It is in the morning when they don't work. In the afternoons they don't come in.

> —Joseph Crescimbeni, Lake City, Florida

• **Cruickshank's Laws.** *Committees:* If a committee is allowed to discuss a bad idea long enough, it will inevitably vote to implement the idea simply because so much work has already been done on it. *Gimme Mine:* No matter how bad the idea, or how poor the results, a program will always be considered a howling success at the local level as long as federal funds continue to pay for it.

> —Ken Cruickshank, the *Florida Times-Union*, Jacksonville, from his June 25, 1978, column

• **Czecinski's Conclusion.** There is only one thing worse than dreaming you are at a conference and waking up to find that you are at a conference—and that is the conference where you can't fall asleep.

> —Adapted from a translation of a letter from Tadeusz Czecinski to a Warsaw newspaper

D

• **Dale's Dictum.** You can't climb a mountain from inside your tent.

> —Dale Wilkins, DW Explorations, Inc., Larkspur, Colorado

• **Dawn's Judgment.** The judgment of any group varies inversely as the square of the number of persons in the group. (If 1 person has x judgment, 2 persons will have $1/4x$ judgment, 10 will have $1/100x$ judgment, etc.)

> —Dawn Barry

• **The Dean-Boyd Law.** Stupidity is intelligence cleverly disguised. *The Beeton Contradiction to the Dean-Boyd Law.* Maybe it's the other way around.

> —Kevin Dean, Don Mills, Ontario, Canada, with Jeff Boyd and Carolyn Beeton

• **Denham's Dictum.** In a given organization, job performance, whether excellent or incompetent, is overlooked providing you conform.

> —Ron Denham, Park Ridge, Illinois

• **Dennis's Principles of Management by Crisis.**
(1) To get action out of management, it is necessary
to create the illusion of a crisis in the hope it will be
acted on. (2) Management will select actions or
events and convert them to crises. It will then over-
react. (3) Management is incapable of recognizing a
true crisis.

> —Gene Franklin, from an article
> of his in *Computers and
> Automation*

• **Density Characteristics of Executives Rising
in an Organization.** Cream rises and sewage floats.
> —Anonymous

• **deQuoy's Observation.** Some of the world's
best work has been done by people who didn't feel
very well that day.

> —Glenna deQuoy, New York,
> New York

• **DeViney's Axiom.** You should always try to
become boss, because otherwise they'll give it to
some other dumbbell.

> —G. H. DeViney, Palatine,
> Illinois

• **Dinshaw's Law No. 1.** It is the incontrovertible
right of the loser to prove that the winner's strategy
was stupid.

> —Dudley Dinshaw, San Jose,
> California

• **Dobson's Dilemma.** (1) Following the rules won't get the job done. (2) Getting the job done is no excuse for not following the rules.
>—From Bob Vopacke,
>Sacramento, California

• **Douskey's Rule Concerning the Odds of Capitalizing on Previous Success.** Sequels never equal.
>—Franz Douskey, Mount
>Carmel, Connecticut

• **Driscoll's Discovery.** The higher one is in a hierarchy the more befuddled one becomes when one attempts to operate the photocopy machine.
>—Robert S. Driscoll, Staten
>Island, New York

• **Dukes's Law.** The most powerful words in marketing are "Watch this!"
>—From James A. Robertson, El
>Paso, Texas, who learned it from
>Carlton Dukes, Dallas, Texas

• **Dull's Advice.** If you can use it, pull it.
>—Joan Dull; from David Finger,
>Wilmington, Delaware, who
>points out that it was created by
>Ms. Dull as a reference to
>pulling strings to get a job, but
>that it has broader applications

E

- **Einstein's Three Rules of Work.** (1) Out of clutter, find simplicity. (2) From discord make harmony. (3) In the middle of difficulty lies opportunity.
  —Albert Einstein, quoted posthumously in *Newsweek*, March 2, 1979

- **Ellenson's Law of Accountability.** Accountability measures the ability to *account*, not the ability to do the job. *Corollary 1:* If one insists on accountability, that is what one will get. *Corollary 2:* If accountability is paramount, that is *all* one will get. *Reductionist Law of Gottas and Shoulds:* There is only one gotta and one should in life: You gotta live with the consequences of your actions, and you should remember that. *Causal Loci:* Blame for any given condition or occurrence will automatically shift until it settles on the least influenceable variable. (E.g., crime may be blamed on social structure, the failure of a business on national economic conditions, etc.)
  —Gerald S. Ellenson, Huntington Beach, California

• **Elsner's Observations.** When you come in late for work, everybody notices; when you work late, nobody notices.

—Raymond F. Elsner, Littleton, Colorado

• **Emmanuel's Law of Customer Satisfaction.** Customer satisfaction is directly proportional to employee satisfaction.

—Daniel Emmanuel, Dallas, Texas

• **Epps's Elevator Law.** A crowded elevator smells different to a short person.

—Buddy Epps; from Don Schofield, Charleston, South Carolina

• **Evelyn's Determination.** Long-range planning works best in the short term.

—Doug Evelyn, Washington, D.C.

• **Evelyn's Rules for Bureaucratic Survival.** (1) A bureaucrat's castle is his desk . . . and parking place. Proceed cautiously when changing either. (2) On the theory that one should never take anything for granted, follow up on everything, but especially those items varying from the norm. The greater the divergence from normal routine and/or the greater the number of offices potentially involved, the better the chance a never-to-be-discovered person will file the problem away in a drawer specifically designed for items requiring a decision. (3) Never say without qualification that your activity has sufficient space, money, staff, etc. (4) Always distrust offices not under your jurisdiction that say they are there to serve you. "Support" offices in a bureaucracy tend to grow in size and make demands on you out of proportion to their service, and in the end require more effort on your part than their service is worth. *Corollary:* Support organizations can always prove success by showing service to someone . . . not necessarily you. (5) Incompetents often hire able assistants.

> —Douglas Evelyn, National Portrait Gallery, Washington, D.C.

• **Everyman's Discovery.** The reliability of any copier is inversely proportional to the number of copies needed.

> —Unknown origin; gathered on WIND Radio in Chicago, Illinois

• **Extended Epstein-Heisenberg Principle.** In a research and development orbit, only two of the existing three parameters can be defined simultaneously. The parameters are: task, time, and resources ($): (1) If one knows what the task is, and there is a time limit allowed for the completion of the task, then one cannot guess how much it will cost. (2) If the time and resources ($) are clearly defined, then it is impossible to know what part of the R & D task will be performed. (3) If you are given a clearly defined R & D goal and a definite amount of money that has been calculated to be necessary for the completion of the task, one cannot predict if and when the goal will be reached. (4) If one is lucky enough and can accurately define all three parameters, then what one deals with is not in the realm of R & D.

—From the article "Uncertainty Principle in Research and Development," in *Journal of Irreproducible Results*, January 1973

F

• **Farkas's Law.** If you want economy, you have to pay for it.

—Unknown origin, but this law is a current tenet of the aerospace cost-analysis community. From Michael Brennan, Pacific Palisades, California, who explains, "The design fabrication and assembly of any new (although in theory less expensive) widget will invariably cost more than just turning the crank and building more of an existing (but in principle more expensive) widget design."

FASSETT'S LAW

• **Fassett's Law.** The first elevator to arrive is going in the wrong direction.

> —Lloyd A. Fassett, M.D.

• **Federal Emergency Advisory.** In case of fire, flee with the same reckless abandon that occurs each day at quitting time.

> —From Bob Levey's column in the *Washington Post,* September 10, 1985, in which he quotes this line from a government bulletin board

• **Ferguson's Rules of Thumb.** (1) When the boss is out, always answer his line second. He is probably on the other line. (Or, the boss never calls on his own line.) (2) The size and severity of the buck passed is inversely proportional to the size of your paycheck. (3) If all the phone lines ring at once, put them all on hold until they hang up. (4) Never answer a person who says, "May I ask a stupid question?" (5) When a caller begins with, "I have a problem," they usually do. When they say, "I have a small problem," it is usually too big for you to handle.

> —Eve M. Ferguson, Washington, D.C.

• **Fetridge's Law.** Important things that are supposed to happen do not happen, especially when people are looking.

—Legend has it that the law was named for a radio engineer in the 1930s named Claude Fetridge, who proposed to the NBC radio network in 1936 that he would be willing to produce a live broadcast of the departure of the swallows from their famous roost at Mission San Juan Capistrano, which, he said, always takes place on St. John's Day, October 23. The network bought the premise and sent a large crew to broadcast the event. The swallows unexpectedly left a day ahead of schedule.

• **Fields's Revelation.** If you see a man holding a clipboard and looking official, the chances are good that he is supposed to be doing something menial.

—Wayne C. Fields, Jr., Newcastle, California

• **The First Law of Corporate Survival.** Keep your boss's boss off your boss's back.

—Unknown origin; from Donald R. Woods.

• **First Law of Government Dynamics.** For every action, there is an equal but opposite inaction.
> —Mike McGuire; from Craig Offutt, Fairfax, Virginia

• **The First Sergeant's Response.** "I'd rather be wrong than look the goddamn thing up."
> —From Brian M. Foley, Wake Island, northern Pacific

• **Fitzloff's Fact.** Organizational consolidation is invariably followed by a minimum increase in administrators of one-third.
> —John F. Fitzloff, Chicago, Illinois

• **Flory's Laws.** (1) The more crap you put up with, the more crap you are going to get. (2) Whenever you put out a trough full of public money, you are going to find some pigs with all four feet in it. (3) As time goes on, everything gets heavier. *Mrs. Flory's Addition to the Third Law.* . . . and farther.
> —K. C. Flory, Oconomowoc, Wisconsin

• **Flowers's Findings.** (1) You are always doing something marginal when your boss drops by your desk. (2) The least important and the most important information gets passed on at the office copy machine. (3) You haven't not worked until you've worked for the government. (4) If someone else's clout depends on your productivity, (s)he'll be on your back.

— T. Camille Flowers, Cincinnati, Ohio

• **Foley's Dicta.** (1) People are generally down on things they ain't up on. (2) If the count goes two strikes against you, cancel the meeting.

— Joe Foley, Kensington, Maryland; quoted in the *Montgomery Journal*, November 5, 1981

• **Fortner's Law.** It takes less time to avoid it than to explain it.

— George A. Fortner, Cincinnati, Ohio

• **Fortune Cookie Message.** Don't blame failures on others. You just didn't work hard enough.

— Found by the late James Thorpe III in an actual fortune cookie

• **Fowler's Law.** In a bureaucracy accomplishment is inversely proportional to the volume of paper used.

— Foster L. Fowler, Jackson, Mississippi; from Alan L. Otten

• **Frand's Laws of Product Development.**
(1) The amount of time necessary to develop a new

product is always one unit of time longer than you think it should be. A one-month project will take one quarter, a two-quarter project will take two years, etc. (2) There is no such thing as a conservative market projection.

—Erwin A. Frand, Industrial Research and Development, January 1983; from Mack Earle

• **Fri's Laws of Regulatory Agencies.** (1) If any agency can regulate, it will. (2) Regulation drives out broad-gauged, long-term thinking.

—Robert Fri, former Environmental Protection Administrator; from Alan L. Otten

• **Fried's Law of Public Administration.** If it's logical, rational, reasonable, and makes good common sense, it's not done. *Corollary:* If it's logical, rational, reasonable, and makes good common sense, don't you do it!

—Steve Fried, Ohio Department of Economic and Community Development, Columbus

• **Frost's Working Rule.** By working faithfully eight hours a day, you may eventually get to be a boss and work twelve hours a day.

—Robert Frost

• **Fullner's Law of Menial Employment.** The more menial a job an individual has, the higher the probability of meeting friends, relatives, and acquaintances while at work. (Discovered while working at a filling station.)
—Randall L. Fullner, San Jose, California

G

• **Gammon's Theory of Bureaucratic Displacement.** In a bureaucratic system an increase in expenditure will be matched by a fall in production. Such systems will act rather like "black holes" in the economic universe, simultaneously sucking in resources and shrinking in terms of "emitted" production. *Or, as restated by Milton Friedman:* In a bureaucratic system, useless work drives out useful work.

> —British physician Dr. Max Gammon, on the completion of a five-year study of the British health system. Discussed by Milton Friedman in his November 7, 1977, *Newsweek* column

• **Gardner's Top-Secret Discovery.** Pentagon motto: Wait, there's a harder way.

> —Martin Gardner, Hendersonville, North Carolina

• **Gene's Guidance.** Grovel; it works.
> —Col. Eugene C. Habisher; from Bob Ackley, Plattsmouth, Nebraska

• **General Electric Razor.** The next time you're in a meeting, look around and identify the yesbutters, the notnowers, and the whynotters. Whynotters move companies.
> —From a 1984 General Electric advertisement

• **Gilbert's Observation.** The surest sign of a crisis is that when you have a major problem, no one tries to tell you how to do your job.
> —Anonymous; from Steve Masse, Concord, Massachusetts

• **Gleason's Advice to Public Administrators.** When leaving office, give your successor three sealed envelopes and instructions to open them in order as crises occur in the new administration. The message in the first should read "blame it on your predecessor," the second should read "announce a major reorganization," and the third should say, "write out three envelopes for your successor."
> —James Gleason, on leaving the post of County Executive, Montgomery County, Maryland. Quoted in the *Montgomery Journal*, November 24, 1978

- **Goodhardt's Forecasting Rule.** Forecasting is never difficult; if it is not easy, it is impossible.

> —Attributed to a Professor Goodhardt; from James Rothman

- **Grabel's Temporary and Freelance Workers Dilemma.** There is always plenty of work when you can't and not enough work when you can.

> —Steven M. Grabel, San Francisco, California

- **Graham's Comment on Forms Design.** There is never enough space for your full address, but always too much for your name.

> —Charles Graham, The Mount, Oxford Road, Gerrards Cross, Bucks, U.K.

- **Gramm's Laws.** (1) It's crowded at the bottom. (2) The early worm gets the bird. (3) You're always on the wrong end of the train.

> —Eugene Gramm, New York, New York

- **Grandpa's Rule on Making a Living.** You can live comfortably by making 1 percent on your money. You buy it for one dollar and sell it for two dollars and you have made 1 percent.

> —Charles W. Steese, Pasadena, California

• **Granger's Advice.** Don't say you've paid your dues until you're at least forty.

> —Bill Granger, *Chicago Tribune*,
> May 27, 1984; from Steve Stine

• **Green's Dictum.** The bottom line is only the tip of the iceberg.

> —Jay Green, Las Cruces, New
> Mexico

• **The Gregory Productivity Axiom.** Any discussion of increasing productivity refers to that of others.

> —Walter Gregory, Milford,
> Connecticut, who explains:
> "Throughout years of participa-
> tion in management meetings
> . . . never once did one of the
> participants ever submit that his
> or her own productivity might
> be increased."

• **Gretzky's Truism.** You miss 100 percent of the shots you never take.

> —Wayne Gretzky. The truism is
> widely quoted but seldom
> applied to hockey.

• **Groebe's Law.** The more complex the problem, the sooner the deadline.

> —Larry Groebe, San Antonio,
> Texas

• **Grold's Law.** If you put your head in the sand, you're going to get shot in the butt.

> —Psychiatrist L. James Grold

• **Gross's Laws.** (1) Good work and mediocre work pay about the same. (2) In the search for the guilty, he who gave the warnings will be remembered. (3) There is always money for the task force. (4) It is better to wear out than rust out. (5) Nothing is worse than a nervous boss, especially when you are the one who is making him nervous.

> —Sidney Gross, Seattle, Washington

• **Grubnick's Process for Effecting Action via Paperwork within the Bureaucracy**. (a) Blitz it with paperwork. (b) Say as little as possible, in as many ways as possible, as verbosely as possible. (c) Always try to tell them what they want to hear. (d) And never, never, never let the facts interfere with your story.

> —David S. Grubnick, Fairbanks, Alaska

• **Guinther's Law of Problem Solving.** It is better to solve problems than crises.

> —John Guinther, in *The Malpractitioners*, Doubleday, 1978

H

- **Haas's Rule.** Everybody's vacations are a nuisance, except one's own.
> —Timothy Haas, Woldingham, Surrey, England

- **Haber's Hypothesis.** For an employee, the number and length of coffee breaks varies directly with the amount of uncompleted work.
> —Meryl H. Haber, M.D., Professor and Chairman of the Department of Laboratory Medicine, University of Nevada, Reno. First published in *The Pathologist,* 1970.

- **Hacker's Law of Personnel.** It is never clear just how many hands—or minds—are needed to carry out a particular process. Nevertheless, anyone having supervisory responsibility for the completion of the task will invariably protest that his staff is too small for the assignment.
> —Andrew Hacker, from *The End of the American Dream,* Atheneum, 1970

• **Hackett's Rule of Planning.** Short-range planning always supersedes long-range planning.
> —David K. Hackett, Knoxville, Tennessee

• **Hale's Hypotheses:** *Black Hole Rule:* Every messy desk contains a black hole, in which papers placed on one side disappear for three months, and then reappear on the other side. *Mail Rule, The:* When you are ready to reply to a letter, you will lack at least one of the following: (a) a pen (or pencil or typewriter), (b) stationery, (c) postage stamp, (d) the letter you are answering. *Vacation Rule:* More happens in the two weeks you are away from the office on vacation than in the fifty weeks you are there. *Nonvacation Corollary:* More happens in the one hour you are at lunch than the seven you are there. *Rule of Occupational Transition:* Don't tell your boss where to go, unless you know where you're going to go. *Hale's Profitability Rule:* The sumptuousness of a company's annual report is in inverse proportion to its profitability that year.
> —The late Irving Hale, Denver, Colorado

• **Hall's Observations.** (1) The word *necessary* seldom is. (2) Most business decisions are based on one critical factor: which method will cause the least paperwork? *Janet's Corollary:* In government, the opposite is true.
> —Keith W. Hall, Harrisburg, Pennsylvania

• **Handel's Proverb.** You cannot produce a baby in one month by impregnating nine women!
> —Sally Handel, New York, New York

• **Hanson's Law of Progress.** Any new form is always longer and more complicated than the one it replaces.
> —Mark D. Hanson

• **Hanson's Treatment of Time.** There are never enough hours in a day, but always too many days before Saturday.
> —Gary W. Hanson, Sioux Falls, South Dakota

• **Harlan's Advice to Hecklers.** Don't start an argument with somebody who has a microphone when you don't; they'll make you look like chopped liver.
> —Writer Harlan Ellison during a speech at the University of New Mexico, ca. 1980, as recalled by Steve Stine

• **Hassell's Modified Maxim.** Hard work never hurt anyone, but then neither did a whole lot of good rest.
> —Richard Arthur Hassell, quoted in a 1984 issue of the *Journal of Irreproducible Results*

• **Haviland's Discoveries.** (1) *Law of Thermodynamics.* Hot-air hand dryers in public washrooms will shut off just as they reach a sufficient temperature to actually begin the drying process and will always have to be restarted. (2) You will never need the full time on the second cycle.
> —James D. Haviland, Halifax, Nova Scotia

• **Hawkeye's Conclusions.** (1) It's not easy to play the clown when you've got to run the whole circus. (2) The tedium here is relieved only by the boredom.
> —Hawkeye Pierce in "M*A*S*H"

• **Hebert's Law of Nonsuccess.** It's lonely at the bottom, too. It's just more crowded.
> —John M. Hebert, New Baltimore, Michigan

• **Hebert's Law of Returning.** If people say, "Oh, here he is" when you get back from wherever, it's not good news.
> —John M. Hebert, New Baltimore, Michigan

• **Heinemann's Law of Executive Recruitment.** The best way to get a good managerial job is to have a good managerial job, no matter how thoroughly you screwed it up.
> —George A. Heinemann, Crystal Lake, Illinois

• **Heller's Myths of Management.** The first myth of management is that it exists. The second myth of management is that success equals skill.
> —Robert Heller, *The Great Executive Dream*, Delacorte, 1972; from John Ehrman

• **Hellman's Product Development Rule.** If you drop something and it doesn't break, mark it heavy duty.
> —Mitch Hellman, Baltimore, Maryland, learned while in new-product development

• **Helmer's Rule of Self-Enlightened Non-resistance.** When dealing with fools, do whatever is necessary to make them happy and get them off your back.
> —John Helmer, *Texas Observer,* September 13, 1985; from Joseph C. Goulden

• **Hempstone's Dictum.** When the federal cow wanders into the paddock, somebody's going to milk it.
> —Syndicated columnist Smith Hempstone, from his column of March 13, 1979

• **Hendrickson's Law.** If a problem causes too many meetings, the meetings become more important than the problem.

> —Anonymous

• **Henry J's Rule.** When your work speaks for itself, don't interrupt.

> —Automotive pioneer Henry J. Kaiser

• **Henry's Law of Annual Reports.** The more rewrites a draft of an annual report is put through, the more the final, accepted draft for printing will match the original draft developed prior to administrative review.

> —C. Henry Depew, Tallahassee, Florida. "Last year," he says, "the annual report I am responsible for producing . . . had thirteen partial and five full rewrites. The end draft . . . almost matched the initial draft."

• **Herbertson's Law of Budgets.** Don't be overly concerned with the cost of paper clips and other office supplies—fire people, and the paper clips will take care of themselves.

> —David M. Herbertson, Sandy, Utah

• **Hewitt's Laws.** (1) Memos marked "Personal and Confidential" are neither. (2) If it looks like jive, it probably is.

> —John H. Hewitt, M.D.,
> Rockville, Maryland

• **Hickman's Guide to Successful Public Relations.** Corn is bacon after it has been processed by a pig.

> —William D. Hickman, Reston,
> Virginia

• **Hinshaw's Hubris.** Gall will get you further than talent. *Hinshaw's Corollary to one of Kenworthy's Laws* (q.v.): To achieve longevity in an organization, be available but not visible.

> —Elton Hinshaw, Secretary-
> Treasurer, American Economic
> Association, Nashville,
> Tennessee

• **Hitchcock's Staple Principle.** The stapler runs out of staples only while you are trying to staple something.

> —Wilbur W. Hitchcock, U.S.
> Consul, Buenos Aires, Argentina

• **Hoffer's Discovery.** The last grand act of a dying institution is to issue a newly revised, enlarged edition of the policies and procedures manual.

> —Philosopher Eric Hoffer; from
> W. J. Vogel

• **Holberger's Rule.** It doesn't matter how hard you work on something; what counts is finishing and having it work.

> —Quoted in Tracy Kidder's *The Soul of a New Machine;* from Shel Kagan

• **Holloway's Law of Downtown Office Buildings.** Whenever you encounter double doors, one will be locked. *Corollary:* The locked door is always the one you try first.

> —Frank Holloway, quoted in Bob Levey's column in the *Washington Post*

• **Holton's Hypothesis.** The length of a presentation is in inverse proportion to its value.

> —Richard Holton, Western Springs, Illinois

• **Horowitz's 435th Law.** Hanging around the watercooler can get you into hot water.

> —Stanley Horowitz, Flushing, New York, from his unpublished collection of aphorisms, *The Nerd's 500 Peachy-Keen Secrets of Success: An Unlikely Guide to the Top*

• **Hubbard's Discovery.** Come good times or bad, there is always a market for things nobody needs.
>—Frank McKinney "Kin" Hubbard (1815–1915)

• **Huddleston's Observation.** Message importance varies directly with the ignorance of the colleague left in charge of your telephone.
>—Dr. Jo H. F. Huddleston, Bracknell, Berkshire, England

• **Hynes's Advice.** When you have a lot of things to do, get your nap out of the way first.
>—Jeremiah Hynes, from his daughter Jo Anderson, Deerfield, Illinois

I

- **Imhoff's Law.** The organization of any bureaucracy is very much like a septic tank—the really big chunks always rise to the top.

> —This first appeared in Thomas L. Martin's *Malice in Blunderland*, McGraw-Hill, 1971, with the following footnote: "Professor John Imhoff, Head of Industrial Engineering, University of Arkansas. A distant cousin, Karl Imhoff, invented the Imhoff Septic Tank of international fame."

- **Indiana Jones's Response to the Next Problem.** "I don't know. I'm making it up as I go along."

> —*Raiders of the Lost Ark;* from Elizabeth Lundren, D.V.M.

• **Industrial Rules.** (1) Interchangeable parts won't. (2) High-pressure oil lines will spray visiting dignitaries.

> —Circulated in the early 1960s at the Raytheon Company in Andover, Massachusetts; from Richard K. Jolliffe of Saskatoon, Saskatchewan, Canada

• **Institutional Input Law.** The wider the interdepartmental consultation on a problem, the less will any agency accept responsibility for the final report.

> —*Washington Star* editorial, February 18, 1979

• **Institutions, Law of.** The opulence of the front-office decor varies inversely with the fundamental solvency of the firm.

> —Unknown origin; from Donald R. Woods

• **The Insurance Catch-22.** If you want it, you can't get it, but if you'll never use it, and don't need it, you can buy all you want.

> —Brian McCombie, "My Turn,"
> *Newsweek*, August 11, 1986

• **Inverse *Peter Principle*.** Everyone rises to his own level of indispensability, and gets stuck here.

> —Dr. Barry Boehm, TRW, during
> a speech before the Special
> Interest Group on Aerospace
> Computing, March 19, 1979. It
> alludes to the 1996 principle cre-
> ated by the late Dr. Laurence J.
> Peter that posited that in any
> hierarchy a person tends to rise
> to his or her level of incompe-
> tence.

• **Invisible People's Rule of Management.** If I tell a man to do what he does not want to do, I am no longer chief.

> —Words of the chief of the
> Invisible People in the movie
> *The Emerald Forest*

• **Issawi's Observation On Cutting Waste from Budgets.** Budget cutters cannot cut waste, because waste is not budgeted.

> —Professor of Near Eastern
> Studies Charles Issawi in the
> *Princeton Alumni Weekly*

J

- **J's Business Maxim.** When perplexed, confused, frustrated, and all else has failed, fall back on the truth. *J's Density Characteristics of Executives Rising in an Organization:* Cream rises and sewage floats.

—Anonymous

- **Jack Frost's Law.** If you need statistics to prove it, it probably wasn't true in the first place.

—From Dr. Joel A. Tobias,
Medford, Oregon, who points
out that Frost was his professor
of medicine at the University of
Pennsylvania

- **Jacobson's Law of Promotion, 1967.** Just when you think you've got the promotion in the bag, some new guy will come along and marry the boss's daughter. *Law of Promotion, 1987:* Just when you think you've got the promotion in the bag, some new gal will come along and marry the boss's son.

—Roberta B. Jacobson,
Greisheim, Germany

• **Jay's Laws of Leadership.** (1) Changing things is central to leadership, and changing them before anyone else is creativeness. (2) To build something that endures, it is of the greatest importance to have a long tenure in office—to rule for many years. You can achieve a quick success in a year or two, but nearly all of the great tycoons have continued their building much longer.

> —Antony Jay, from *Management and Machiavelli,* Holt, Rinehart and Winston, 1967

• **Jennifer's Secretarial Law.** Only when the final draft of the document has been typed up and printed will the boss remember a crucial point that must be added to the middle of it.

> —Jennifer Feenstra, Montreal, Quebec, Canada

• **Jesson's Law of Office Supply Dynamics.** There is never a paper clip on the floor when you need one.

> —Dick Jesson, San Francisco, California

• **Just's Rule of Monthly Meetings.** Monthly meetings always last two hours, regardless of the number and importance of the items on the agenda. This is because if there is little to be discussed the participants will spend more time discussing each point because there is no pressure to move things along. . . . [T]he time available . . . is controlled by the same factor which limits meetings to two hours when there is much to discuss, which is that when you have reached two hours there are always a few people who are being called by nature, and usually the chairperson is one of them.

—Rev. Christian F. Just, Euclid, Ohio

K

• **Kagan's Theorem of the Hidden Agenda.**
There is always more going on than you think.
Corollary: And it's always worse than you imagine.
> —Shel Kagan, Canoga Park,
> California

• **Kahn's Laws.** (1) Vice presidents never call back. (2) Entrepreneurs always call back.
> —Steve Kahn in the *Wall Street Journal*, March 21, 1984

• **Karl's Laws of Bureaucratic Paper Flow.** (1) Every bureaucracy generates paperwork in a logarithmic fashion. A one-page directive will inevitably lead to a five-page guideline, a ten-page procedure and a twenty-five-page report. (2) Any attempt to clarify the information contained in a directive, guideline, or procedure will increase the amount of paperwork in each of the subsequent steps.
> —Edward Karl, Urbana, Illinois

- **Kass's Plagiarism.**
  Those who can—do.
  Those who cannot—teach.
  Those who can do neither—inspect.
  > —Nicholas E. Kass, Lt. Col.,
  > USAF (Retired), Fort Walton
  > Beach, Florida; a play on George
  > Bernard Shaw's line about
  > teachers

- **Kelly's Law.** An executive will always return to work from lunch early if no one takes him.
  > —Unknown origin, "Laws to
  > Live By," *The Farmers' Almanac*

- **Key to Status:** $S = D.K.$ S is the status of a person in an organization, D is the number of doors he must open to perform his job, and K is the number of keys he carries. A higher number denotes a higher status. Examples: The janitor needs to open 20 doors and has 20 keys ($S = 1$), a secretary has to open two doors with one key ($S = 2$), but the president never has to carry any keys since there is always someone around to open doors for him (with $K = 0$ and a high D, his S reaches infinity).
  > —Psychologist Robert Sommer,
  > from his paper "Keys, Kings and
  > Kompanies"

- **Klein's Law of Utilitarian Discipline.** You always have to keep a few screwups in the organization. Otherwise, what would we use as a yardstick to

judge our flawless performance?
>—William S. Klein, Springfield,
>Illinois

• **Knight's Rules of Business.** (1) Do business only with people whose word you consider to be as good as their contract. (2) Then get it in writing anyway.
>—Gary Knight, Baton Rouge,
>Louisiana

• **Koolman's Clerical Truth.** Everything can be filed under "miscellaneous."
>—Ron Koolman, Golf Manor,
>Ohio

• **Kopcha's Commercial Reality.** Often the smartest thing to do is the most obvious thing to do; it is also often the hardest thing to sell.
>—Stephen C. Kopcha,
>Bloomfield Hills, Michigan.
>From the University of Missouri
>alumni magazine, via Bob Skole.

• **Kramer's Rules.** (1) Monday is a depressing way to spend one-seventh of your life. (2) If you're at the top of the ladder, cover your ass; if you're at the bottom, cover your face. (3) Whatever is dreaded arrives promptly.
>—Professor Mary Kramer,
>Lowell, Massachusetts

• **Kroeger's Law of Public Relations Account Management.** The client on the smallest budget is the one that requires the most attention and account service time.

> —Judi Kroeger, Allentown, Pennsylvania

• **Krukow's Observation on Public Life.** You haven't lived until some ten-year-old kid calls you a hemorrhoid.

> —Baseball player Mike Krukow; collected by John Rush, Austin, Texas

L

- **Lada's Important Definitions for the Bureaucratic Environment.** *Committee:* A work group created with the main purpose of finding and articulating reasons why a new idea will not work, or, failing that, why adoption of the new idea will cause more anguish within the institution than the idea's benefits are worth. *Policy:* A written statement, ordinarily using as many words as possible, to articulate an institutional position on a subject in a manner vague enough to permit multiple contradictory interpretations. *Task Force:* A group organized to present the illusion of progress without the inconvenience of actually moving the institution forward.
>   —Stephen C. Lada, Wayne,
>   Michigan

- **Lang's Law of Bureaucratic Entropy.** The total amount of bureaucracy in an organization can never decrease. It can only increase—and usually does.
>   —Tony Lang, Imperial College,
>   London, England

- **Lawrence's Laws.** (1) Paperwork is inversely proportional to useful work. (2) In any bureaucracy, the triviality of any position can be derived by counting the number of administrative assistants.

> —Bob Ackley, T. Sgt., USAF,
> Plattsmouth, Nebraska

• **Lee's Law of Business Competition.** Always remember to keep your swash buckled.

> —Gerald Lee Steese, Long
> Branch, California

• **Levinson's Lesson.** Many people have come to expect too much of work. Work is work, no matter how you slice it.

> —Dr. Harry Levinson, of *The
> Levinson Letter,* quoted in
> *Behavioral Sciences Newsletter,*
> July 25, 1983

• **Liebman's Laws of Auto-motion.** (1) If you get a great parking spot, you've probably shown up on the wrong day. (2) The later you are the heavier the traffic conspiracy.

> —Sam Liebman, Montreal,
> Quebec, Canada

• **Loewe's Rules of Governance.** (1) If the government hasn't taxed, licensed, or regulated it, it probably isn't worth anything. (2) The ability of the government to create money is likened to a child's desire to change the rules of a game he is losing.

> —Donald C. Loewe, Chicago,
> Illinois

• **Loftus's Latest Collection.** *John Henry's Rule:* It is a lot more fun to sing about hard work than to actually perform hard work. *Loftus's Sixth Rule of Government:* When it comes to government programs, no matter how noble the purpose or grand the design, implementation is everything. *Loftus's Seventh Rule of Government:* Government programs never go away; they only change their titles. *Loftus's Observation on Meetings:* Meetings that you chair are infinitely better than those that you merely attend. *Loftus's Advice for the Workplace:* Research has repeatedly shown that the best response to the supervisor's query "Got a minute" is "No."

> —Mel Loftus, Alexandria, Virginia

LOFTUS'S ADVICE for the WORKPLACE

• **Lopez's Iron Law of Corporations.** In a business, everyone is expendable, but some are more expendable than others.

> —Marsha J. Lopez, *New York Times*, January 25, 1986

• **Loren's Basic Principle for Bureaucratic Survival.** The appearance of a bureaucracy is infinitely more important than its function.

> —Unknown origin; from John A. Mattsen

• **Lowell's Law.** You will always find the easiest, fastest, most economical way to do any project around the time you are finishing it.

> —Jeffrey Lowell, Cleveland Heights, Ohio

M

- **MacPherson's Working Formula.** The number of interruptions received during a work period is proportionate to the square of the number of employees occupying an office—thus, one person in an office = one interruption per hour; two in an office = four interruptions per hour; three people = nine per hour, etc.

> —Ian MacPherson, Regina, Saskatchewan, Canada

- **Magary's Principle.** When there is a public outcry to cut the deadwood and fat from any government bureaucracy, it is the deadwood and fat that does the cutting.

> —John T. Magary, Royal Oak, Michigan

- **Mahon's Silicon Valley Rule.** Don't let your employees do to you what you did to your former boss.

> —Tom Mahon, *Charged Bodies: People, Power and Paradox in Silicon Valley;* from Jack Limpert

• **Marcus's Law.** Never divorce the boss's daughter (or son).

> —Stanley Marcus, Dallas, Texas, from his book *Quest for the Best*

• **Marshall's Distinction.** A government could print a good edition of Shakespeare's works, but it could not get them written.

> —Economist Alfred Marshall

• **The Mary Principle.** If many individuals remain too long at their level of incompetence they will destroy the organization, because their presence demonstrates to others that competence is not a prerequisite for success.

> —Unknown origin; from J. Thomas Parry, Rockford, Illinois, but it is a play on the *Peter Principle,* created by the late Laurence J. Peter, whose great finding held that everyone eventually rises to their own level of incompetence.

• **Masefield's R & D Rule.** The principal function of an advanced design department nowadays is to keep up with the public relations department.

> —Peter Masefield, British Aircraft Managing Director, quoted in Leonard Louis Levinson's *Webster's Unafraid Dictionary,* Collier Books, 1967

• **Maverick's Observation.** "Work is all right for killing time, son, but it's no way to make a living."
> —Bret Maverick, the character from the venerable TV show "Maverick"; from Don Coles of St. Louis, Steve Stine, and Bernard L. Albert

• **McCarthy's Adage.** The only thing that saves us from the bureaucracy is inefficiency. An efficient bureaucracy is the greatest threat to liberty.
> —Eugene McCarthy, quoted in *Time*, February 12, 1979

• **McGovern's Law.** The longer the title, the less important the job.
> —Robert Shrum, who was one of George McGovern's speechwriters, recalled this law for Alan L. Otten of the *Wall Street Journal*. McGovern discovered the law in 1960, when President Kennedy tried to persuade him that being director of the Food for Peace Program was a more influential job than secretary of agriculture. McGovern's Law works for many jobs: senator, president, judge, CEO, coach, king.

• **McNaughton's Rule.** Any argument worth making within the bureaucracy must be capable of being expressed in a single declarative sentence that is obviously true once stated.

> —The late John McNaughton, a government national security expert. It was sent to Alan L. Otten by Harvard political scientist Graham Allison.

• **Melcher's Law.** In a bureaucracy every routing slip will expand until it contains the maximum number of names that can be typed in a single vertical column, namely, twenty-seven.

> —Daniel Melcher

• **Miller's Law.** All costs walk on two legs.

> —Arjay Miller; from Hal Hoverland, Dean, California State College, San Bernardino

• **Mills's Correlation.** If you pay peanuts, you get monkeys.

> —James Mills in his novel *The Underground Empire;* from Charles D. Poe

• **Moran's Theorem for the Self-Employed.** You spend the first half of your career wondering if people will buy your services and the second half won

dering when they'll get around to paying for them.
—Frank J. Moran, Los Angeles,
California

• **Moynihan's Maxim.** Whenever any branch of the government acquires a new technique that enhances its power in relation to the other branches, that technique will soon be adopted by those other branches as well.
—Senator Daniel P. Moynihan; from Alan L. Otten

• **Murphy's Observation on Organizations and Management.** Amazing! How things so wrong can last so long.
—Buz Murphy, Haddonfield, New Jersey

N-O

• **NASA Truisms.** (1) Research is reading two books that have never been read in order to write a third that will never be read. (2) A consultant is an ordinary person a long way from home. (3) Statistics are a highly logical and precise method for saying a half-truth inaccurately.

> —From a file in the NASA archives on "Humor and Satire"

• **Nathan-Dommel Law of Federal Grants.** Given the chance, governments will spread benefits so as to provide something for everybody.

> —Richard Nathan and Paul Dommel, "Understanding the Urban Predicament," *The Brookings Bulletin*, 14:1–2, 1977

• **Neudel's Laws.** (1) Any organization created to unite a proliferation of splinter groups inevitably becomes another splinter group. (2) Any person hired by a bureaucracy to respond to public complaints has no power to remedy them. *Corollary:* The only people worth talking to in a bureaucracy are the ones who never deal with the public. (3) The most important information in any communication is the most likely to be either garbled by the communicator or misunderstood by the recipient.

> —Marian Henriquez Neudel,
> Chicago, Illinois

NASA TRUISMS

• **Newlan's Truism.** An acceptable level of unemployment means that the government economist to whom it is acceptable still has a job.

> —Anonymous; from John W.
> Gustafson, who has no idea who
> Newlan was or is

• **Offut's Unnamed Law on the Development of Statistics.** Garbage in; gospel out.

> —Craig Offut, Fairfax, Virginia

• **Ormerod's Rule.** Don't try to think like the top until you are the top.

> —David Ormerod, Middletown,
> Ohio

P-Q

• **Packard's Telephone Frustration.** You place an urgent call to somebody requiring a quick answer. You are told he is tied up for a moment and will call right back. You put off other calls, meetings, and lunch but you never get the call you so desperately need until it is too late.

> —L. H. Packard, Westmount, Quebec, Canada

• **Palmer's Comment on Retirement.** It really bothers me to think I may never throw a home-run pitch again.

> —Jim Palmer, reflecting on his forced retirement from the Baltimore Orioles, quoted in *Sports Illustrated*

• **Paula Principle.** In a hierarchy women are not allowed to rise to their level of incompetence.

—This discovery was announced in a paper "The Paula Principle and Women's Liberation," by Benjamin Mittman, Evanston, Illinois. Mittman examined the *Peter Principle* ("In a hierarchy every employee tends to rise to his level of incompetence") and asked the following: "[If] the Peter Principle were universally true, why has not society crashed into the chasm of incompetence? How can institutions, governments, and business survive? What has prevented the Peter Principle from destroying civilization? What mitgating influence has saved us?" The answer is the Paula Principle, which has "sustained society."

• **Pentagon Sign.**
THEY TOLD HIM THE JOB COULDN'T BE DONE. HE ROLLED UP HIS SLEEVES AND WENT TO IT. HE TACKLED THE JOB THAT COULDN'T BE DONE—AND HE COULDN'T DO IT.

—Unknown origin; found at the Department of Defense

• **Petroff's 27th Law of Hierarchical Behavior.**
Humility decreases with every promotion, and disappears completely at the vice-presidential level.
Corollary: Arbitrariness increases with every promotion, and becomes absolute at the vice-presidential level.

> —John N. Petroff, Dhahran,
> Saudi Arabia

• **Phillips's Planning Rule.** Remember, the future is written in sand—the past in concrete.

> —Sherry A. Phillips, Wichita,
> Kansas

• **Proposal-Writing Rules.** (1) Never mention money. "Resources" is the prime substitute, although "allocations" and "appropriations" are also popular. (2) Fluff up a proposal with the sort of euphemisms that bestow an aura of importance without revealing anything specific.

> —Louis Kaplan, planner, quoted
> in *Newsweek*, May 6, 1968

R

- **Rabbe's Revision.** The check's in the fax machine.
>>> —Don Rabbe, Lincoln, Nebraska

- **Radcliffe's Rule.** There's no such thing as a single call to a federal agency.
>>> —Charles W. Radcliffe, Minority Counsel, House Committee on Education and Labor, quoted in the *National Report for Training and Development,* September 24, 1982; from Mollie N. Orth

- **Radovic's Rule.** In any organization, the potential is much greater for the subordinate to manage his superior than for the superior to manage his subordinate.
>>> —Igor Radovic, in *How to Manage the Boss; or, The Radovic Rule,* M. Evans, 1973

- **Ralph's Rule.** If you can't get somebody else to do it for you, it's not worth doing at all.
>>> —Dave Pawson, Dallas, Texas

• **Randall's Reminder.** The closest to perfection a person ever comes is when he fills out a job application form.

> —Stanley Randall, quoted by
> Patrick Ryan in *Smithsonian*

• **Randall's Rule of Economic Indicators.** Increased productivity occurs when the number of unemployed not working is greater than the number of employed who are not working.

> —Warren Randall, Stony Brook,
> New York

• **Rathbun's Generalization.** Generalizations and value judgments are all bad. *Rathbun's Rule:* There is no harder nor more thankless taskmaster than the self-employed.

> —J. M. Rathbun, M.D.,
> Cumberland, Wisconsin

• **Reasons Why Not (50 Handy-Dandy Excuses).** (1) We've never done it before. (2) Nobody else has ever done it. (3) It has never been tried before. (4) We tried it before. (5) Another company (person) tried it before. (6) We've been doing it this way for twenty-five years. (7) It won't work in a small company. (8) It won't work in a large company. (9) It won't work in our company. (10) Why change—it's working OK. (11) The boss will never buy it. (12) It needs further investigation. (13) Our competitors are not doing it. (14) It's too much trouble to change. (15) Our company is different. (16) The ad department says it can't be done. (17) The sales department says it can't be sold. (18) The service department won't like it. (19) The janitor says it can't be done. (20) It can't be done. (21) We don't have the money. (22) We don't have the personnel. (23) We don't have the equipment. (24) The union will scream. (25) It's too visionary. (26) You can't teach an old dog new tricks. (27) It's too radical a change. (28) It's beyond my responsibility. (29) It's not my job. (30) We don't have the time. (31) It will obsolete other procedures. (32) Customers won't buy it. (33) It's contrary to policy. (34) It will increase overhead. (35) The employees will never buy it. (36) It's not our problem. (37) I don't like it. (38) You're right, but . . . (39) We're not ready for it. (40) It needs more thought. (41) Management won't accept it. (42) We can't take the chance. (43) We'd lose money on it. (44) It takes too long to pay out. (45) We're doing all right as it is. (46) It needs committee study. (47) Competition won't like it. (48) It needs sleeping on. (49) It won't work in this department. (50) It's impossible.

—This list has been popular in engineering circles for years. The earliest published appearance was in *Product Engineering,* July 20, 1959. It was supplied to the magazine by E. F. Borisch of the Milwaukee Gear Co.

• **Retsof's Rush-Hour Blizzard Law.** If there is a suitable morning snowstorm, an employee will leave after the storm to go to work. Given an equivalent afternoon snowstorm, the employee will leave before the storm to go home.

> —John C. Foster, Columbus, Ohio. For reasons that are unclear, Foster spells his name backward when composing laws.

• **Rickover's Rule.** If you have a choice of sinning against God or the bureaucracy, sin against God, because He will forgive you, and the bureaucracy will not.

> —Advice from the late Admiral Hyman Rickover, cited in the May 10, 1993, issue of *NuclearFuel*

• **Rigsbee's Principle of Management.** Your brightest, sharpest new employees are the first to leave your organization—as the cream rises to the top it will be skimmed off.

> —Ken Rigsbee

• **Robertson's Rules of Hierarchy.** The more directives you issue to solve a problem, the worse it gets.

> —Jack Robertson, *Electronic News,* first quoted in *New Engineer,* November 1976

• **Robson's Rule.** Learning always occurs after the job is finished.

> —Thayne Robson, University of Utah; from William D. Hickman

• **Rogers's Boss Law.** There will always be beer cans rolling on the floor of your car when the boss asks for a lift home from the office.

> —Dennis Rogers

• **Rules of the Office.**
If it rings, put it on hold;
If it clanks, call the repairman;
If it whistles, ignore it;
If it's a friend, take a break;
If it's a boss, look busy;
If it talks, take notes;
If it's handwritten, type it;
If it's typed, copy it;
If it's copied, file it;
If it's Friday, forget it!!!

> —From David Broome, Phoenix, Arizona

• **Rupp's Rule.** If you demonstrate competence, it becomes part of your Job Description.

> —Sandra K. Rupp, R.N., Monticello, Florida

S

- **Samuelson's Corollary.** Public bureaucracy breeds private bureaucracy.

> —Robert J. Samuelson,
> *Washington Post*, June 6, 1978.
> As he explains, "The more gov-
> ernment expands, the more it
> stimulates a vast supporting
> apparatus of trade associations,
> lawyers, lobbyists, research
> groups, economists, and consul-
> tants—all trying to shape the
> direction of new federal regula-
> tions and spending programs."

- **Sarge's Astute Observations of Human Behavior #37.** When your boss says, "You don't have to if you don't want to," he means, "You *have* to even if you don't *want* to."

> —Tom Gill, from "Beetle Bailey,"
> December 29, 1994

- **Savage's Business Lesson.** Forgive and Remember.

> —Joy Savage, Pacific Grove,
> California

• **Seymour's Beatitude of Bureaucracy (on the treatment of employee complaints).** The first time you're a disgruntled employee. The second time you're a pain in the ass. The third time you're a nut.
—John Seymour, Bayonne, New Jersey

• **Shapiro/Kaufman Law.** The lag in American productivity is directly related to the steady increase in the number of business conferences and conventions.

—Walter Shapiro and Aleta Kaufman in their article "Conferences and Conventions: The $20-Billion Industry That Keeps America from Working," *Washington Monthly*, February 1977

• **Skole's Rule of Antique Dealers.** Never simply say, "Sorry, we don't have what you are looking for." Always say, "Too bad, I just sold one the other day."
—Robert Skole, reporter, Stockholm, Sweden, and Boston, Massachusetts

• **Smith's Law.** The economy is strong only to those who are well off. *Colaterally:* The unemployment rate is never very good to those out of work.
—Gerald L. Smith, Homeland, California

• **Smith's Principle of the Displaced Hassle.** To beat the bureaucracy, make your problem their problem.

—Marshall L. Smith

• **Snyder's Law.** In any situation involving more than one person doing similar jobs, the important information will be given to the person not involved in the project, and he will forget to pass it along, as it does not involve him.

—Daniel K. Snyder, Pearl City, Hawaii, who offered this example: "While researching material for the completion of a job, my cohort was informed that the job was canceled, a fact that I was informed of two days later upon completion of the job."

• **Springer's Law.** Whenever someone you know, or someone you do business with, moves to a new location, it's always farther away.

—Sherwood Springer, Hawthorne, California

• **Stark's Laws.** (1) The demand is greatest for the item that just ran out of stock. (2) Of contracting: The most problems will occur on jobs farthest from the shop.

—Paul W. Stark, Kansas City, Kansas

- **Stein's Simplified Economic Theory.** The money stays the same; the pockets just keep changing.

> —Author Gertrude Stein; from William Lurie, Bellevue, Washington

- **Straus's Axioms.** (1) Everything the government touches turns to solid waste. (2) After the government turns something to solid waste, it deregulates it and turns it into natural gas.

> —V. Michael Straus, Washington, D.C.

- **Strother's Discovery.** The loftier the ideals of an organization, the dirtier the infighting.

> —George B. Strother, Madison, Wisconsin

- **Szymcik's Universal Law of Experts.** An expert is not someone who is often right, as opposed to a nonexpert; each is wrong about the same percent of the time. But the expert can always tell you why he was wrong; so you can always tell the difference.

> —Rev. Mark Szymcik, Leominster, Massachusetts

T

- **Tansik's Law of Bureaucratic Success.**
Success in a bureaucracy depends not so much on
whom you please, but on whom you avoid making
angry. *Corollary:* To succeed, concentrate not on
doing great things but on the avoidance of making
mistakes.

> —David A. Tansik, Associate
> Professor, University of Arizona

- **Taylor's Discovery.** In any organization there
are only two people to contact if you want results—
the person at the very top and the person at the very
bottom.

> —Warren E. Taylor, Burlington,
> North Carolina

- **Thomas's Rules of the Game.** (1) No matter
how well you do something, someone won't like it.
(2) No matter how trivial the assignment, it is always
possible to build it up to a major issue. (3) A good,
illegible signature is a key to success.

> —Robert H. Thomas,
> Farmington, Michigan

- **Thompson's Publication Premise.** The probability of anyone reviewing a document in full diminishes with the number of pages.

  —Charles I. Thompson III, Port Jefferson Station, New York

- **Thomson's Law.** Ten percent of your subcontractors will give you 90 percent of your aggravation.

  —Kenneth D. Thomson, San Francisco, California

- **Tom's Caca and the Fan Theory.** Some of us dance because we like the music. The rest of us are just dodging the falling debris.

  —Tom English

- **Toomey's Rule.** It is easy to make decisions on matters for which you have no responsibility.

  —Jim Toomey, the St. Louis Cardinals, St. Louis, Missouri

- **Trauring's Discovery.** Technical reports are expanded from outlines, so that aides can recondense them for executive use.

  —Mitchell Trauring, Los Angeles, California

- **Truths of Management.** (1) Think before you act; it's not your money. (2) All good management is the expression of one great idea. (3) No executive devotes effort to proving himself wrong. (4) Cash in must exceed cash out. (5) Management capability is always less than the organization actually needs. (6) Either an executive can do his job or he can't. (7) If sophisticated calculations are needed to justify an action, don't do it. (8) If you are doing something wrong, you will do it badly. (9) If you are attempting the impossible, you will fail. (10) The easiest way of making money is to stop losing it.

—Robert Heller, *The Great Executive Dream,* Delacorte, 1972

• **Turk's Laws of Traffic.** (1) It is always rush hour. (2) "Fast lanes" do not exist. (3) An accident in one lane will slow all lanes, regardless of their number and direction.

—Brian Turk, Phoenix, Arizona

UPWARD-MOBILITY RULE

U-V

• **Uncle Ed's Rule of Managerial Perception.**
You always think the boss is a son of a bitch until
you're the boss. *Uncle Ed's Rule of Thumb:* Never
use your thumb for a rule. You'll either hit it with a
hammer or get a splinter in it.
—Edward Karl, Urbana, Illinois

• **Underwood's Distinction.** The extent to which
a service organization has become a bureaucracy is
measured by the degree to which useless work has
driven out useful work. In pure bureaucracy all
work is useless and tends only to perpetuate the
bureaucracy. In pure service all work is useful, altru-
istic, and of greater ultimate value than the organization itself.
—The Rev. John F. Underwood,
King of Prussia, Pennsylvania

• **Upward-Mobility Rule.** Don't be irreplaceable.
If you can't be replaced, you can't be promoted.
—Desk sign; unknown origin;
collected from radio call-in show

• **Vancini's Discovery.** In a bureaucracy, good ideas go too far.

> —John Vancini, Brooklyn
> Center, Minnesota

• **Van Roy's Laws of Work.** (1) *Van Roy's Basic Law:* Honesty is the best policy—there's less competition. (2) *Van Roy's Rule of Empowerment at Work:* Never agree with your boss until he says something. (3) *Van Roy's Limitations Rule of Work Complexity:* Anything that is simple to do is never easy to accomplish.

> —Bruce W. Van Roy, Vienna,
> Virginia

• **Vaughan's Rule of Corporate Life.** The less important you are on the table of organization, the more you'll be missed if you don't show up for work.

> —The late Bill Vaughan of the
> *Kansas City Star*

• **Veeck's Law of Enforced Humility.** When you've run as fast as you can up the highest mountain you can find, you will find something or somebody waiting at the top to deflate you.

> —The late baseball man Bill
> Veeck, from his book *Veeck as in
> Wreck*

• **Vietinghoff's Precept.** He who controls the forms controls the program.

> —William F. Vietinghoff, Space Shuttle Main Engine Systems, Rockwell International, Canoga Park, California

• **Vogel's Observation of Office Behavior.** When an executive on vacation picks up pebbles and small shells from the beach and flippantly tosses them into the air, it is merely a continuation of his career-long habit of zipping rubber bands at the back of the head of his busy secretary.

> —Arthur R. Vogel, Evanston, Illinois

W

- **Wallner's Rule.** If a thing is worth doing, hire it out.

  —Marilyn Wallner, Carmichael, California

- **Walters's Law of Management.** If you're already in a hole, there's no use to continue digging.

  —Roy W. Walters, Roy Walters Associates, Glen Rock, New Jersey

- **Warren's Warning.** If the boss calls, get his name.

  —James Warren, Las Cruces, New Mexico

- **West's Laws.** (1) *West's Basic Law:* The difficulty in arranging a meeting varies as the square of the number of people involved. (2) *The Law of Professionalism:* The value of the service or product you buy increases as the cube of its quality and professionalism and rarity. (To put it another way, the baseball player who bats .360 is worth more than twice as much as the player who bats .180. In fact, the .360 hitter is in Hall of Fame territory, while the

.180 hitter is on the verge of flunking out of the business altogether.)

> —Richard E. West, Rye, New
> Hampshire

• **Wicker's Law.** Government expands to absorb revenue—and then some.

> —Tom Wicker, *New York Times*

• **Wilgus's Warning.** Always slow down for Dead Man's Curve.

> —Neal Wilgus, Albuquerque,
> New Mexico

• **Willis's Law of Public Administration.** In any federal management report, the recommendations that would result in actual savings will be rejected, but the rejection will be "balanced" by the enthusiastic acceptance of those that increase costs.

> —Bennett Moser Willis,
> McLean, Virginia, former Chief
> of Management, U.S.
> Department of Justice

• **Woehlke's Law.** Nothing is done until nothing is done.

> —Richard A. Woehlke, Sutton, Massachusetts. A few examples from the man who discovered the law: (1) Middle managers can never get the people they need for a job as long as they continue to muddle through by means of overtime, ulcers, and superhuman effort. But when enough people quit in frustration so that the job is not finished, upper management will approve the hiring of the necessary people. (2) Ditto for salaries. (3) The energy crisis [substitute your favorite crisis] will worsen until the whole house of cards collapses. Then and only then will effective measures be taken.

• **Woodruff's Work Rule.** *Everybody* works for the sales department.

> —Jeff Woodruff; from Marshall L. Smith

_X-Y-Z_

• **X's Boss Discoveries.** (1) The boss does not sleep—he/she rests. (2) The boss is never late—he/she is delayed. (3) The boss never leaves work early—his/her presence is required elsewhere. (4) The boss is never sarcastic—he/she is witty. (5) The boss is not hard to work for—he/she is a stern taskmaster.

—Unknown origin

• **Young's Law.** Nothing is illegal if one hundred businessmen decide to do it.

—Andrew Young

• **Zimmerman's Law.** Regardless of whether a mission expands or contracts, administrative overhead continues to grow at a steady rate.

—Charles J. Zimmerman

• **Zisla's Discoveries.** (1) A good administrator tries to do as little as possible; a bad administrator tries to do as much as possible. (2) Don't concern yourself too much with the "bottom line." There will be a new one tomorrow or even before. (3) It doesn't matter how many catastrophes you survive, living will still kill you. (4) It is possible to paint zebra stripes on an elephant but it won't do much good as a disguise: The zebras will know it is still an elephant, and even though they will be puzzled, maybe even confused, so will the other elephants.

—Harold Zisla, South Bend, Indiana

— *Special Bonus Sections* —

Glossary of Important Business Terms

- **Activate.** To make copies and add more names to the memo.
- **Advanced Design.** Beyond the comprehension of the ad agency's copywriters.
- **All New.** Parts not interchangeable with existing models.
- **Approved, Subject to Comment.** Redraw the damned thing.
- **Automatic.** That which you can't repair yourself.
- **Channels.** The trail left by interoffice memos.
- **Clarify.** To fill in the background with so many details that the foreground goes underground.
- **Conference.** A place where conversation is substituted for the dreariness of labor and the loneliness of thought.
- **Confidential Memorandum.** No time to mimeograph/photocopy for the whole office.
- **Consultant.** Someone who borrows your watch to tell you what time it is—then walks away with the watch.
- **Coordinator.** The person who has a desk between two expediters (see Expedite).

• **Developed After Years of Intensive Research.** Discovered by accident.

• **Expedite.** To confound confusion with commotion.

• **Forwarded for Your Consideration.** You hold the bag for a while.

• **FYI.** Found Yesterday. Interested?

• **Give Someone the Picture.** To make a long, confused, and inaccurate statement to a newcomer.

• **Give Us the Benefit of Your Present Thinking.** We'll listen to what you have to say as long as it doesn't interfere with what we've already decided to do.

• **In Conference.** Nobody can find him/her.

• **In Due Course.** Never.

• **Infrastructure.** (1) The structure within an infra. (2) The structure outside the infra. (3) A building with built-in infras.

• **It Is in Process.** So wrapped up in red tape that the situation is almost hopeless.

• **Let's Get Together on This.** I'm assuming you're as confused as I am.

• **Meeting.** A mass meeting by the masterminds.

• **Note and Initial.** Let's spread the responsibility for this.

• **Policy.** We can hide behind this.

• **Program.** Any assignment that cannot be completed by one telephone call.

• **See Me.** Come down to my office, I'm lonely.

• **Sources.**
   Reliable Source—The person you just met.

Informed Source—The person who told the person you just met.

Unimpeachable Source—The person who started the rumor originally.

• **Top Priority.** It may be idiotic, but the boss wants it.

• **Under Active Consideration.** We're looking in the files for it.

• **Under Consideration.** Never heard of it.

• **We Are Making a Survey.** We need more time to think of an answer.

• **We Will Look into It.** By the time the wheel makes a full turn, we assume you will have forgotten about it too.

• **Will Advise in Due Course.** If we figure it out, we'll let you know.

　　　　—Compiled from several sets of "Office Definitions" retrieved from real offices

Job Performance Evaluation

Performance Factor	Outstanding	High Satisfactory
Quality	Leaps tall buildings with a single bound.	Needs running start to jump tall buildings.
Timeliness	Is faster than a speeding bullet.	Only as fast as a speeding bullet.
Initiative	Is stronger than a locomotive.	Is stronger than a bull elephant.
Adaptability	Walks on water consistently.	Walks on water in emergencies.
Communication	Talks with God.	Talks with angels.
Relationship	Belongs in general management.	Belongs in executive ranks.
Planning	Too bright to worry.	Worries about future.

Satisfactory	Low Sastisfactory	Unsatisfactory
Can only leap small buildings.	Crashes into buildings.	Cannot recognize buildings.
Somewhat slower than a bullet.	Can only shoot bullets.	Wounds self with bullets.
Is stronger than a bull.	Shoots the bull.	Smells like a bull.
Washes with water.	Drinks water.	Passes water in emergencies.
Talks to himself.	Argues with himself.	Loses those arguments.
Belongs in rank and file.	Belongs behind a desk.	Belongs with competitor.
Worries about present.	Worries about past.	Too dumb to worry.

—all unattributed

• **Job Performance** *(What the Description Means)*. The military uses fitness reports in the evaluation of personnel performance. The following comes from an unofficial U.S. Navy document but applies to general use.

Average: Not too bright.
Exceptionally well qualified: Has committed no major blunders to date.
Active socially: Drinks heavily.
Zealous attitude: Opinionated.
Character above reproach: Still one step ahead of the law.
Unlimited potential: Will tick until retirement.
Quick thinking: Offers plausible excuses for errors.
Takes pride in his work: Conceited.
Takes advantage of every opportunity to progress: Buys drinks for superiors.
Forceful and aggressive: Argumentative.
Indifferent to instruction: Knows more than his seniors.
Stern disciplinarian: A bastard.
Tactful in dealing with superiors: Knows when to keep his mouth shut.
Approaches difficult problems with logic: Finds someone else to do the job.
A keen analyst: Thoroughly confused.
Not a "desk" man: Did not go to college.
Expresses himself well: Speaks English.
Spends extra hours on job: Miserable home life.
Conscientious and careful: Scared.

Meticulous in attention to detail: A nitpicker.
Demonstrates qualities of leadership: Has a loud voice.
Judgment is usually sound: Lucky.
Maintains professional attitude: A snot.
Keen sense of humor: Has a vast repertory of dirty jokes.
Strong adherence to principles: Stubborn.
Gets along extremely well with superiors and subordinates alike: A coward.

Afterwords

This is the first in a series of books that will help describe elements of the real world through laws, rules, principles, and maxims.

Needless to say, the Director is ever eager to collect new laws and hear from readers. Write in care of:

The Murphy Center
Box 80
Garrett Park, MD 20896-0080

Shortly after the first book, *The* [original] *Official Rules*, was published in 1978 the writer got a letter from a good woman from Pagosa Springs, Colorado, who said: "Once discovered, *The Official Rules* is like sex, indispensable."

Ever since then, the Director has relished the task of going to the mailbox for the Center's mail.

One of the benefits that accrue to those who help The Murphy Center with its research is their appointment as a Fellow of The Murphy Center. The value of such a title should be reckoned by the fact that it can be given only by the Director and cannot be bought (at least not cheaply) and cannot be taken away by anyone but the Director (who has yet to decomission a Fellow). There are now so many Fellows that it would be impossible to list all of them at the end of the book—as was the practice in earlier Center publications.

In addition, there is a select group of people who have contributed so much to the work of the Center over the last twenty years that they have achieved the rank of Senior Fellow. They cannot be thanked enough, but I will do it one more time: the late Theodore C. Achilles, Joseph E. Badger, Nancy Dickson, the late Russell Dunn Sr., Fred Dyer, M. Mack Earle, John Ehrman, Tom Gill, Joseph C. Goulden, Shel Kagan, Martin Kottmeyer, Edward Logg, Herbert H. Paper, the late Charles D. Poe, Frank S. Preston, Conrad Schneiker, Bob and Monika Skole, Marshall L. Smith, Robert D. Specht, Steve Stine, Gregg Townsend, Neal Wilgus, Bennett Willis Jr., Jack Womeldorf, Steve Woodbury, and Donald R. Woods.

Index

Lada's, Lang's, Lawrence's (2), Loewe's, Loftus's, Loren's, Magary's, McCarthy's, McNaughton's, Melcher's, Neudel's (1, 2), Rickover's, Samuelson's, Seymour's, Smith's Principle, Tansik's, Taylor's, Underwood's, Vancini's

Business/Business Terms. Blumenthal's, Green's, J's, Knight's, Savage's, Young's

Business Meals. Condon's, Kelly's

Capitalism. Cooke's

Career. Boyle's (1), Joe Cooch's (3)

Cash Flow. Boston's

Change. Allen's Rule, Blake's

Church. Chilton's

Circus. Hawkeye's (1)

Civil Service. Civil Service Maxim

Clothing. Brozik's (2)

Clowns. Hawkeye's

Clutter. Einstein's, Hale's

Coalitions. Clay's

Coffee/Coffee Breaks. Haber's

Coincidence. Joe Cooch's (1)

Committees. Carlisle's, Cruickshank's (1), Lada's

Commodities. Adkins's

Communication/Communications. Allcock's, Celine's (2), Neudel's, Snyder's

Company/Corporation Policy. Ackley's Latest, Addis's Business (1)

Competence/Incompetence. Ackley's Axiom, Joe Cooch's (15), Inverse Peter Principle, Rupp's, Wallner's

Competition. Lee's

Complaints. Combs's, Seymour's

Conclusions. *Cavalry Journal*, Clay's, Hawkeye's

Conferences/Conventions. Bethell's, Czecinski's, Shapiro/Kaufman

Conformity. Denham's

Consistency/Constants. Air Force Inertia, Allen's Rule, Bernstein's

Consolidation. Fitzloff's

Consultants/Consulting. Brennan's (3), NASA

Contradictions. Mahon's

Control. Collins's

Controversy. Allen's Tenet

Corporations. Lopez's

Correctness. Air Force Inertia

Cost Control. Connolly's, Cooke's

Cost of Living. Brennan's (2)

Costs. Connolly's, Miller's, Zimmerman's

Crap. Flory's (1)

Crises. Boyd's, Branch's, Dennis's, Gilbert's, Gleason's

Customers. Byars's (2), Emmanuel's

Deadlines. Groebe's

Decisions/Decision-making. Arnold's, Boyd's, Cason's (4),

Management. Ackley's Axiom,
Aman's, Brennan's (3),
Cavanagh's, Dennis's,
Heinemann's, Heller's,
Invisible People's, Kramer's
(2), Murphy's, Radovic's,
Rigsbee's, Truths, Walters's,
Zisla's (1)
Manpower. Bone's
Marketing. Butler's Marketing,
Dukes's, Frand's (2),
Hubbard's, Skole's,
Woodruff's
Medicine. Advertising
Admonition
Meetings. Cason's (4), Foley's
(2), General Electric Razor,
Hendrickson's, Just's,
Loftus's, West's (1)
Memorandum. Brown's Laws,
Hewitt's
Memory. Addis's Business (1)
Merit. Advice to Officers (2)
Military. Advice to Officers,
Anonymous's Contribution,
Joe Cooch's
Miscalculations. Boyle's (1, 2)
Mistakes. Ackley's Latest,
Boyle's (6), The First
Sergeant's, Tansik's
Mondays. Kramer's
Money. Grandpa's, Stein's,
Truths (1, 4, 10)
Motivation. Tom's

National Security.
Anonymous's Contribution,
Celine's (1)
Navy. Allen's Rule

Necessity/Needs. Berla's,
Hall's (1), Jesson's
Nothing. Woehlke's

Observations. Blumenthal's,
Coolidge's, deQuoy's, Elsner's,
Gilbert's, Hall's, Krukow's,
Maverick's
Objectives. Anonymous's
Reminder
Office Buildings. Holloway's
Office Machines/Equipment.
Bender's, Driscoll's,
Everyman's, Flowers's (2),
Hitchcock's, Rabbe's
Office Rules. Addis's Business
(1), Dobson's, Ferguson's,
MacPherson's, Rules
Officials. Caffyn's, Fields's
Opinion. Allen's Tenet
Opportunity. Einstein's (3)
Orders. Advice (3)
Organizations. Murphy's,
Radovic's
Overhead. Zimmerman's

Paper/Paperwork. Brown's
Law, Brown's Law of
Business Success, Brown's
Laws, Fowler's, Grubnick's,
Hall's (2), Hanson's Law,
Karl's, Lawrence's (1),
Vietinghoff's
Paper Clips. Anthony's (5),
Herbertson's, Jesson's
Parachuting. Brown's
Aphorism
Parking. Liebman's
Patsys. Buffett's

Burdg's, Chism's, Flory's (3),
Fortner's, Hanson's
Treatment, Haviland's (2),
Kramer's (3), Lowell's
Titles. McGovern's
Traffic. Liebman's, Turk's
Trouble. Boren's
Trust. Amis's
Truth/Truisms. Gretzky's,
Koolman's, NASA, Newlan's
Turkeys. Alan's
Typing. Bender's

Unemployment. Coolidge's,
Newlan's, Smith's
Upward Mobility. Upward-
Mobility Rule

Vacations. Haas's, Hale's

Victory. Amundsen's

Warnings. Warren's, Wilgus's
Waste. Issawi's, Straus's
Watercooler. Horowitz's
Weekends. Busch's
Wheels. Arnold's
Winning. Canfield's
Wisdom. Addis's Admonitions
Women. Paula Principle
Work. Benchley's,
Crescimbeni's, Einstein's,
Elsner's, Frost's, Gross's (1),
Haber's, Hassell's, Henry J's,
Holberger's, Kramer's,
Levinson's, Loftus's,
Maverick's
Worth. Brennan's